What I Like

Holidays

Liz Lennon

W
FRANKLIN WATTS
LONDON • SYDNEY

I love going on holiday. It's fun to visit new places.

I pack everything I need in my suitcase.

I like travelling by train.

There's lots to see out of the window.

Whoosh!

Sometimes we fly to
another country for
our holiday.

There are lots of aeroplanes to see at the airport.

Zooooom!

Last year we went to visit a city.

This year we're going walking in the countryside.

Sometimes we go camping.

I like sleeping in a tent.

The campsite is by the sea.

Hotels are also fun to stay in on holiday.

I like playing with Dad
in the swimming pool.

I like to take my bike on holiday.

Mum and Dad bring
their bikes too.

Wheeee!

We eat out at cafés and restaurants on holiday.

masalabay

LUNCH SPECIAL

SHEEK KEBAB £6.95
2 STICKS OF KEBAB SERVED WITH MIXED SALAD

FISH 'N'CHIPS £6.75
LARGE COD OR HADDOCK SERVED WITH CHIPS 'N' PEAS

CHIKEN TIKKA WRAP £6.95
SUCCULENT PIECES OF CHICKEN TIKKA WRAPED
NAN BREAD AND SERVED WITH MIXED SA

CHICKEN OR VEG NOODLES

CHICKEN OR BEEF BURGER £5.25 £6.50
SERVED WITH CHIPS AND A SALAD GARNISH

MORE CHOICE AVAILABLE
FROM OUR LUNCH AND ALACRTE MENU

I get to try new foods.
Sometimes I like
them and sometimes
I don't!

I try other new things on holiday too. Watch me ski.

I tried pony-riding once. Sometimes the pony went too fast!

The best thing
about holidays ...

We look at our photos to
remember all the fun we had.

About this book

Holidays, for those children lucky enough to have them, are an important part of a child's world - helping them to find out about places, foods and experiences outside their normal lives. Looking at and talking about the pictures is a good starting point for discussing holidays. Here are some ideas for further talking points:

Getting ready What do they take with them on holiday? What's the most important item?

Travelling What is their favourite way to travel? Why? Have they ever been on a plane - what was it like? What could they see from the window?

Different places What different kinds of holiday can they think of - seaside, city, etc?

Which is their favourite? Where have they already been? Where would they like to go?

Where to stay What different places can we stay in - tents, cottages, hotels, caravans, with family etc? Which relatives have they been to stay with? What sort of place would they like to stay in?

New experiences What new things have they done on holiday? What were they like? what else would they like to do?

Going home Are they sad or happy to go home at the end of a holiday? What do they look forward to about going home? Do they look at photos of their holidays? What other ways can they think of to help them remember a good holiday?

First published in 2011
by Franklin Watts

Copyright © Franklin Watts 2011

Franklin Watts
338 Euston Road
London NW1 3BH

Franklin Watts Australia
Level 17/207 Kent Street
Sydney, NSW 2000

All rights reserved.

Dewey number: 394.2'6
ISBN: 978 1 4451 0469 0

Printed in China

Series Editor: Sarah Peutrill
Art Director: Jonathan Hair
Series Designer: Paul Cherrill
Picture Researcher: Diana Morris
Consultants: Karina Philip
and Deborah Cox

Franklin Watts is a division of
Hachette Children's Books,
an Hachette UK company.

www.hachette.co.uk

Every attempt has been made to
clear copyright. Should there be any
inadvertent omission please apply to
the publisher for rectification.

Picture credits: Alamy: Image Source
12; Robert Stainforth 16. Istockphotos:
Ana Abejon 3; Mark Bowden 15;
Christopher Futcher 23; Maria Pavlova
5; Sasha Fox Walters 19; Jianying Yin
17. Shutterstock: AISPIX 22; Norman
Chan 8; Flashon Studio 14; Gorilla
9, 18; JaySi 1, 21; Peter Kirilov 11;
Kokhanchikov 10; Daleen Loest 13;
Robyn Mackenzie 2br; Rob Marmion
front cover; MC_PP 7; oliveromg 20;
Regien Paassen 2b; PHB.cz (Richard
Semik) 2cr; Tiorna 2cl; Vincius
Tupinamba 2t; upthebanner 2bl;
Nikola Vukojevic 4. Superstock: Blend
Images 6.t